PICTURE LIBRARY

HAMSTERS

PICTURE LIBRARY
HAMSTERS

Norman Barrett

Franklin Watts

London   New York   Sydney   Toronto

Franklin Watts Inc
387 Park Avenue South
New York
NY 10016

Printed in Italy

Designed by
Barrett and Weintroub

Photographs by
Marc Henrie
Pat Morris
Mary Evans Picture Library
Oxford Scientific Films
Survival Anglia

Illustration by
Rhoda and Robert Burns

Technical Consultant
David Alderton

Library of Congress Cataloging-in-Publication Data

Barrett, Norman S.
    Hamsters/Norman Barrett; [illustration by Rhoda & Robert
Burns].
        p.   cm.   (Picture library)
    Summary: Describes various types of hamsters, their feeding,
social, and reproductive habits, and life cycles. Includes
suggestions for raising hamsters domestically.
    ISBN 0-531-14032-6
    1. Hamsters—Juvenile literature.   [1. Hamsters.]   I. Burns,
Rhoda, ill.   II. Burns, Robert, ill.   III. Title
QL737.R638B385   1990
599.32′33—dc20   89-21518
                                                        CIP
                                                        AC

Contents

Introduction   6
Looking at hamsters   8
Kinds of hamsters   10
Domestic hamsters   14
Life and habits   20
Keeping hamsters   24
The story of hamsters   28
Facts and records   30
Glossary   31
Index   32

Introduction

Hamsters are small members of the rodent family. They have loose-fitting skin, bright eyes, and feet that are good for grasping. They are agile and acrobatic.

Golden hamsters make popular pets. There are other species (kinds) of hamsters that live in the wild. The common hamster is a much bigger animal, and is regarded as a pest in some parts of the world.

△ The golden hamster is a popular pet. Its normal color is reddish-brown on the back, white streaks on the cheeks and a grayish-white belly.

Both short-haired and long-haired varieties of golden hamster are kept as pets throughout Europe and the United States. Breeders have also developed a variety of coat colors in addition to that of the original golden hamster.

△ A variety of coat colors has been developed in pet hamsters. But even these gray ones are still known as golden hamsters.

Looking at hamsters

Hamsters vary in size from the giant European hamster, the size of a rabbit, to the tiny dwarf hamster, no bigger than a mouse.

Common (European) hamster

Golden (Syrian) hamster

Dwarf (Dzungarian) hamster

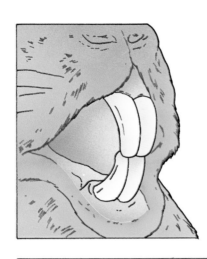

◁ Long incisor teeth grow continuously and have to be worn down by gnawing

▷ The hamster fills its cheek pouches with food to take back to its burrow or store in a hiding place in its cage

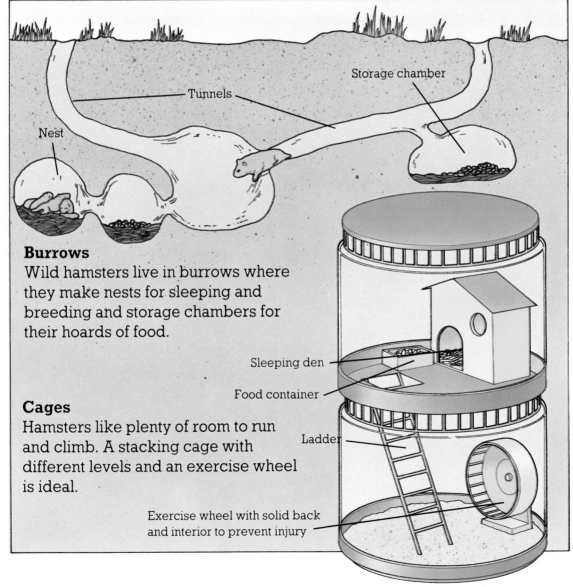

Storage chamber

Tunnels

Nest

Burrows
Wild hamsters live in burrows where they make nests for sleeping and breeding and storage chambers for their hoards of food.

Cages
Hamsters like plenty of room to run and climb. A stacking cage with different levels and an exercise wheel is ideal.

Sleeping den

Food container

Ladder

Exercise wheel with solid back and interior to prevent injury

Kinds of hamsters

There are more than 20 species of hamsters. The golden, or Syrian, hamster is most widely bred in captivity. It has been only rarely seen in the wild.

The Chinese hamster and the smaller dwarf, or Dzungarian, hamsters have also been domesticated. They are similar in appearance, but not in habits and behavior, to the golden hamster.

▽ The golden hamster is no longer found in the wild.

The only other species sometimes kept in captivity is the common, or European, hamster – but not as a pet. These creatures, about the size of rabbits, cannot be tamed. Even when kept in zoos, they might have to be handled with gloves reinforced by steel mesh!

The common hamster is regarded as a pest because it destroys crops. But in some places it is trapped for food or fur.

△ The common hamster may look cute, but it is an aggressive creature. It lives on the grassy plains of central Europe and the Soviet Union. It hibernates in winter and stores masses of grain in its deep burrows. About the size of a rabbit, it breeds just as fast.

▷ Dzungarian hamsters, called dwarf Russians as domesticated pets, are dark gray with a white belly. They come from the cold deserts of western Asia – Siberia, Manchuria and northern China – where the black stripe on their back may turn white in winter to camouflage them in the snow.
They make gentle pets, but breed only in their natural color.

Domestic hamsters

Pet hamsters have been bred in a variety of coat patterns and colors. By carefully selecting mating pairs, breeders have been able to bring out certain features to produce new colors and markings.

Colors of pet hamsters range from the light brown of the original golden hamster to white. Satin-coated and long-haired hamsters have also been bred.

△ The terms used for hamster varieties are not always truly descriptive, and sometimes you have to be an expert to tell the difference. These are young "yellow" hamsters.

▷ A rust banded
hamster.

▽ A golden dominant
spotted hamster.

◁ A dark golden hamster.

▷ A tortoiseshell and white satin-coated hamster. Satin coats are fine and glossy, with a satin sheen. The coarser hair has been bred out, so the coats are not waterproof.

▽ A smoke pearl hamster.

These very light-colored hamsters have quite different shades. The usual hamster eye coloring is black, but many varieties can be bred with ruby, or red, eyes.

◁Lilac, with black eyes.

▽Blonde, with ruby eyes.

△A rex-coated
hamster. Rex fur is
dense and curly, and
even the whiskers are
curled.

▷A long-haired white
hamster. Most varieties
of golden hamster can
be bred with long hair.
The coat is soft and
silky to the touch.

Life and habits

Female hamsters carry their young in their body for about 16 days. They give birth usually to 6 or 7 babies, but litters can range from 2 to 15.

Common hamsters have two or three litters a year. But golden hamsters, in captivity, may give birth once a month.

The young are helpless at birth, but leave their mother after three or four weeks.

△ A litter of five young hamsters on a nest of shredded paper.

Among themselves, hamsters are unsociable animals and tend to fight when they meet. After leaving their mother, the young prefer to live alone. Their only contact with other hamsters is for mating. This is as true for hamsters in captivity as for the common hamster and other species in the wild.

Hamsters are most active at night. The common hamster hibernates (goes into a deep sleep) during the winter months.

▽ A dwarf hamster in the wild. Its pouches are puffed out with food, which it will eventually take back to its burrow.

In the wild, hamsters live on seeds, grain, fruits, green vegetation, and living prey such as insect larvae. The common hamster might even prey on larger creatures, such as mice and lizards.

Hamsters keep themselves and their living area clean. They use their "hands," or front paws, to clean themselves and to hold food and bedding material. Healthy pet hamsters usually live two to four years.

▽ Hamsters sometimes get angry, especially if teased or disturbed. But they make very little vocal sound.

△ A golden hamster
nosing around among
some tid-bits. Hamsters
like all kinds of seeds
and nuts, and are
particularly fond of
sunflower seeds.

▷ Hamsters eat by
holding their food in
their front paws.

23

Keeping hamsters

Hamsters are easy to care for. They do not take up much room, but their cage should be kept in a warm place, away from drafts. Never house more than one hamster in a cage.

Although hamsters do not run or jump, they should not be allowed to roam freely. They are curious animals and likely to scamper off a tabletop and hurt themselves, or get lost under the floorboards.

△ When choosing a hamster, look for signs of good health – a solid, well-fed body, soft, silky fur and prominent eyes. Activity is also a sign of a healthy hamster.

△ A hamster's cage should have an absorbent floor covering of wood shavings and a sleeping compartment with bedding material such as hay or shredded paper. A supply of clean water should always be available.

◁ Hamsters are friendly toward humans. Getting to know them calls for patience at first, but they will soon enjoy being petted. They should be held gently but firmly.

△ Hamsters need plenty
of exercise. They enjoy
exercise wheels, and it
is a good idea to put one
in the cage.

◁ Food should be
placed in a heavy dish
that the hamster cannot
tip over or chew.

▷ Long-haired hamsters need grooming. Their coat must be brushed regularly, with a gentle hairbrush or even a soft toothbrush.

▽ Even the healthiest hamsters might need a visit to the vet, often for overgrown claws or incisor teeth.

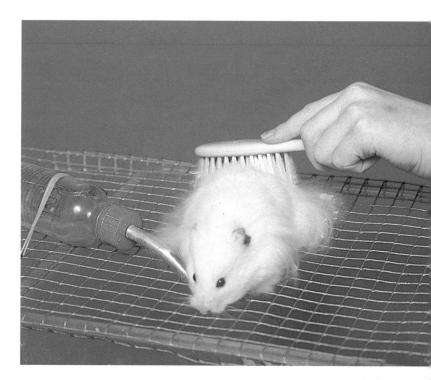

The story of hamsters

△ An old engraving shows common hamsters raiding a field of wheat in central Europe.

The fiercest hamster

The common hamster has never been tamed. These fierce animals originally inhabited the steppes (grassy plains) of eastern Europe and western Asia, but moved into central and western Europe to live around farmland. They were once kept for their fur and meat, but were found very difficult to handle.

They are hoarders, with a reputation for stealing crops. In some places traps are set for these hamsters. But the use of pesticides and mechanized farming methods has had a greater effect on their population.

Discovering the Syrian hamster

The golden hamster was first identified in 1839, in Syria, by an English naturalist called Waterhouse, who sent dead specimens to a London museum. The species was thought to be extinct until, in 1930, an expedition from the Zoology Department of the Hebrew University at Jerusalem found a mother and 12 young in a burrow near Aleppo, Syria.

The young hamsters were taken back to Jerusalem, where

three of them survived and began to breed the following year. Few wild golden hamsters have been seen since, and we know that every tame golden hamster in captivity today is descended from these three animals.

Hamsters as pets

The first hamsters were brought to England in 1931, and hamsters arrived in the United States in 1938, when some were sent to the Public Health Service at Carville, Louisiana. For many years only scientists bred them, for use in laboratory experiments. Then, in the mid-1940s, it was discovered that hamsters made good pets. They soon became extremely popular. By 1950, in the United States alone there were an estimated 100,000 golden hamsters.

Breeding

The first variation from the natural hamster color was found in 1948. From that time, breeders have carefully chosen their breeding stock to "fix" new characteristics and colors. In the wild, odd-colored animals would not survive, but in captivity they can be used as breeding stock to create new varieties.

△ A long-haired albino, the result of careful breeding. These and all other golden hamsters are descended from three animals found in the wild in 1930.

Showing

Sometimes, hamster shows are organized by county fairs. The animals, under various categories, are judged according to set standards of color, markings, fur, size and condition. Many shows have special classes for novices and juniors, in which a pet hamster stands a good chance of winning a prize.

△ The hamster show cage may be opened easily and the exhibit removed.

Facts and records

Naming the hamster

The hamster's name reflects its best known characteristic. It comes from a German word, "hamstern," which means "to hoard."

The scientific name for the golden hamster, *Mesocricetus auratus*, means "middle-sized golden mouse."

Champion hoarders

One of the most remarkable hoarders of all the hamsters is the Korean gray hamster from China. Second only to the common hamster in size, it has been known to store more than a bushel of grain, some 27 kg (60 lb). Chinese peasants have survived famine by digging up the Korean gray's stores.

Not to be outdone, the common hamster may store as much as 90 kg (200 lb) of seeds, roots and plants in its burrow – that's 100 times its own weight!

Pouches

Hamsters use their cheek pouches for collecting food and material for their nests. When fully extended, the pouches can hold an amount of food equal to about half the size of the hamster itself.

Size

Hamsters range in size from the common hamster, 20 – 28 cm (8 – 11 in) tall, to the dwarf hamster, 5 – 10 cm (2 – 4 in). The golden hamster averages about 15 cm (6 in).

△ The dwarf hamster may measure only 5 cm (2 in) from head to tail.

Shortest pregnancy

The hamster has the shortest pregnancy, or period of gestation (the time a female carries its unborn babies), of any mammal – 16 days.

A thousand days

The normal life span of a healthy pet hamster is about 1,000 days. This is only 2 years 9 months. Hamster rarely live for more than 3 years.

Glossary

Albino
An animal that has white coloring because it cannot produce pigment (coloring substance). An albino is completely white except for red eyes.

Camouflage
Coloring that helps an animal to blend in with its surroundings.

Cheek pouches
Internal pouches that extend from a hamster's cheeks to its shoulders. The hamster fills its cheek pouches by putting food or material for its nest into its mouth. Sometimes a mother hamster will carry her babies in the pouches.

Hibernate
To go into a deep sleep for the winter months. A hibernating animal protects itself against the cold and can live off the fat stored in its body.

Incisor teeth
Front teeth used for cutting and gnawing. These grow continuously and may become too long if the hamster does not get enough hard things to chew on. They may be clipped by a vet.

Litter
The baby animals born at one time. Hamster litters average 6 or 7 babies.

Naturalist
A person who studies wildlife.

Pesticide
A chemical that crops are treated with in order to poison pests that would destroy them.

Prey
Animals used as food by other animals.

Satin coat
A coat in which the coarser hair has been bred out, leaving a glossy sheen.

Species
A particular kind of animal or plant. Animals of the same species breed young of that species.

Varieties
Animals of the same species but with different features, such as color, texture or pattern of coat, length of hair, or color of eyes. Varieties are also known as variations.

Index

albino 29, 31

birth 20
breeder, breeding 7, 14, 29
burrow 9, 11, 21, 30

cage 9, 24, 25, 26, 29
camouflage 12, 31
cheek pouches 9, 21, 30, 31
Chinese hamster 10
claws 27
color 6, 7, 12, 14, 18, 29
common hamster 6, 8, 11, 20, 21,
    22, 28, 30

dwarf hamster 8, 10, 12, 21, 30
Dzungarian hamster 8, 10, 12

European hamster 8, 11
exercise wheel 9, 26
eyes 6, 18, 24

feet 6
fight 21
food 9, 21, 22, 23, 26, 30
fur 11, 24, 28, 29

golden hamster 6, 7, 8, 10, 14, 15,
    17, 19, 20, 23, 29, 30
grain 11, 22, 30
grooming 27

hibernate 11, 21, 31
hoarding 9, 30

incisors 9, 27, 31

Korean gray hamster 30

life span 22, 30
litter 20, 31
long-haired hamster 7, 14, 19, 27

name 30
naturalist 28, 31
nest 9, 20, 30

paws 22, 23
pesticide 28, 31
pet 6, 7, 11, 12, 14, 22, 24, 25, 29, 30
pregnancy 30
prey 22, 31

rex-coated hamster 19

satin-coated hamster 14, 17, 31
showing 29
size 8, 29, 30
species 6, 10, 31
storage chamber 9
Syrian hamster 8, 10, 28

teeth 9, 27

varieties 29, 31
vet 27

water 25
whiskers 19

young 20, 21, 28

32